EVANGELICAL BELIEF

A short explanation of the
Doctrinal Basis of the
Universities and Colleges
Christian Fellowship

Inter-Varsity Press

Inter-Varsity Press
38 De Montfort Street, Leicester, LE1 7GP, England

© Inter-Varsity Press, 1988

Unless otherwise stated, Scripture quotations in this publication are from the Holy Bible, New International Version. Copyright © 1973, 1978, 1984, International Bible Society. Published by Hodder & Stoughton.

First edition 1935
Second edition 1951
Third edition 1961
Fourth edition 1973
Fifth edition 1988 (based on the revised Doctrinal Basis of 1981)

British Library Cataloguing in Publication Data

Universities and Colleges Christian Fellowship
    Evangelical belief. – 5th ed.
    1. Christian doctrine
    I. Title
    230
ISBN 0 85110 246 8

Set in Linotron Clearface
Typeset in Great Britain by Parker Typesetting Service, Leicester
Printed in Great Britain by Cox & Wyman Ltd, Reading

Inter-Varsity Press is the book-publishing division of the Universities and Colleges Christian Fellowship (formerly the Inter-Varsity Fellowship), a student movement linking Christian Unions in universities and colleges throughout the United Kingdom and Republic of Ireland, and a member of the International Fellowship of Evangelical Students. For information about local and national activities write to UCCF, 38 De Montfort Street, Leicester, LE1 7GP.

CONTENTS

PREFACE

The Universities and Colleges Christian Fellowship, and the Christian Unions in the student world, have the privilege of standing for the faith of the Bible, which God has entrusted to the people. The Bible brings us the gospel (how we may know God), and our Christian calling (how we may walk with him and please him).

If we are to know God's Word in a living and joyful way, and if we are to tell others about Christ, we need to understand what it teaches. The Fellowship's Doctrinal Basis summarizes the main truths of the Bible, and this booklet helps us to understand them.

When student leaders, staff and committee members of the UCCF assent to the Doctrinal Basis, we accept the statements in their plain sense, always understanding that we need to test them by Scripture. This booklet does not offer detailed or binding judgments, but an explanation of how the Doctrinal Basis is generally understood by those who subscribe to it.

This edition follows a long line of previous editions, dating from 1935. It has been prepared in the light of the rewording of certain clauses of the Doctrinal Basis which took place in 1981. No substantial change in the meaning was made, but at certain points the wording needed to be made clearer. Some things taken for granted in earlier years need clearer statement in today's world. At each point the new wording only makes more explicit what was at least implied before.

ROBIN WELLS
UCCF General Secretary

INTRODUCTION

Why have a doctrinal basis?

Stability
Imagine a gigantic horse-chestnut tree. In the summer it is a vast green mass; only leaves are visible. If you didn't know any better you might think that it was a giant foam-rubber shape. But in winter you see a skeleton of bare branches and you can see what holds all that summer foliage together. Without that framework it would be just a heap of leaves, blown away by the first breeze.

Understanding our Christian faith is rather like that. To be strong and vigorous as Christians, able to stand against the devil's tricks and to help others to do the same, we need to have some sort of intellectual understanding of what the Bible teaches – of what God has to say to us. This will strengthen us against what Paul calls 'every wind of teaching' (Ephesians 4:14) in this confused world, where we meet with all sorts of views and schools of thought calling us to follow them.

Effective witness
It's not only for the sake of stability that we need to understand what we believe. It's also essential for effective evangelism. Sixty years ago the modern student Christian Unions were founded on the

conviction that they were called to 'confessional witness'. We need to witness to the Lord Jesus Christ among our fellow students. But we need to be sure that what we say in our witness is true to the gospel, to the truth we confess.

Writing about the meaning of the death of Christ, John Stott has said, 'The better people understand the glory of the divine substitution, the easier it will be for them to trust in the Substitute.'[1] Paul saw evangelism as being a clear and faithful explanation of the truths about the Lord Jesus. We need the same concern in our evangelism today.

Understanding

The New Testament makes this point in a number of ways. Take the word 'light', for example. 'Light' is used to illustrate different things such as joy and purity. But one of its important meanings is a knowledge of the truth. Darkness is the opposite – ignorance and mental blindness. That is why there is so much emphasis in the New Testament on teaching. Jesus taught, and he sent his apostles to do the same. The church's early pattern in Acts 2:42 shows this. The Acts and the Letters confirm it – warning, teaching, opposing wrong teaching.

The New Testament writers hold this before us again and again. Paul warns his hearers of the dangers of wrong teaching 'with tears' (Acts 20:19, 31). He wasn't just a philosophical crank; he wasn't just 'cerebral'. Some people may complain that his letters are heavy reading, but what he had to say was for him a matter of life or death. Paul and the others knew that valid experience and worthwhile relationships must have a solid foundation on things that are really true! So it's not just a quarrelsome spirit that makes Jude urge his readers to 'contend for the faith' (Jude 3). In fact, if we shrink from that call we disobey the Bible!

Health

There's another word that Paul uses that helps us see why truth is so important. He writes to Timothy, towards the end of his life, and urges Timothy to keep as the pattern of sound teaching whatever he has heard from Paul. Perhaps that word 'sound' has a slightly strange ring to us today. It simply means 'healthy', or 'health-giving'. To be spiritually healthy and useful to God, we need the nourishing diet that the apostolic teaching gives us.

We should be under no illusions: ignorance, vagueness and confusion are spiritually unhealthy! The 'pattern of this world' that Paul wrote to the Roman church about (Romans 12:2) includes an indifference to truth. That pattern carries a spiritual health-warning!

The history of the church over the centuries shows the importance of the truth. The apostles' warnings about the danger of wrong ideas are proved valid again and again. God's people are always tempted to wander from the foundation of New Testament teaching and when they do they come to grief. 'The Christian church, whether universal or local, is intended by God to be a *confessional* church. . . . However hostile the spirit of the age may be to an outspoken confession of the truth, the church has no liberty to reject its God-given task.'[2]

9

Of course, we can 'major on minors'. We can put so much emphasis on secondary or uncertain views that we can't live in peace with those who disagree with us. We will always find that Christians differ on many less important things. If we cannot keep these in perspective in relation to the fundamentals it becomes difficult for others to have fellowship with us. And interdenominational witness in the student world becomes impossible. A seventeenth-century preacher, Jeremy Taylor, once commented, 'I would that men would not make more necessities than God made, which indeed are not many'.

But what God has given to us as necessary truths we may not modify, weaken or abandon. We have a body of revealed truth in which our personal faith may rest. It is our intellectual and spiritual anchorage.

In the New Testament more is expected of leaders than of other members of the church fellowship. Today, too, most churches look for greater doctrinal understanding from those responsible for leadership than from ordinary members. And in UCCF, the Committee members and officers of the Fellowship are required by the Constitution to sign the Doctrinal Basis. Membership of the Christian Unions, however, is open to all who can affirm their faith in 'Jesus Christ as my Saviour, my Lord and my God' or some similar short declaration of faith.

The Docrinal Basis of the Universities and Colleges Christian Fellowship of Evangelical Unions (UCCF) is meant to give a short and balanced summary of fundamental points of the gospel, particularly for the limited purposes of the Christian

Unions. It focuses on the beliefs common to evangelicals, the truths on which we can unite in presenting the gospel. The Doctrinal Basis reads as follows:

The doctrinal basis of the Fellowship shall be the fundamental truths of Christianity, as revealed in Holy Scripture, including:

a. The unity of the Father, the Son and the Holy Spirit in the Godhead.

b. The sovereignty of God in creation, revelation, redemption and final judgment.

c. The divine inspiration and infallibility of Holy Scripture as originally given, and its supreme authority in all matters of faith and conduct.

d. The universal sinfulness and guilt of human nature since the fall, rendering man subject to God's wrath and condemnation.

e. The full deity of the Lord Jesus Christ, the incarnate Son of God; his virgin birth and his real and sinless humanity; his death on the cross, his bodily resurrection and his present reign in heaven and earth.

f. Redemption from the guilt, penalty and power of sin only through the sacrificial death once and for all time of our representative and substitute, Jesus Christ, the only mediator between God and man.

g. Justification as God's act of undeserved mercy, in which the sinner is pardoned all his sins, and accepted as righteous in God's sight, only because of the righteousness of Christ

imputed to him, this justification being received by faith alone.

h. The need for the Holy Spirit to make the work of Christ effective to the individual sinner, granting him repentance toward God and faith in Jesus Christ.

i. The indwelling of the Holy Spirit in all those thus regenerated, producing in them an increasing likeness to Christ in character and behaviour, and empowering them for their witness in the world.

j. The one holy universal Church, which is the Body of Christ, and to which all true believers belong.

k. The future personal return of the Lord Jesus Christ, who will judge all men, executing God's just condemnation on the impenitent and receiving the redeemed to eternal glory.

These eleven clauses do not present the whole of the Bible's teaching. We need everything that Scripture teaches, and to go further in an understanding of Christian doctrine. Some of the books in the list for further reading on pages 94–96 may help in this.

But doctrine is not just to be studied. God's purpose is to reconcile us to himself, and also to produce in us a heart which loves and worships him as Father, and a life which reflects his character.

In the light of what he has been teaching Peter asks, 'What kind of people ought you to be? You ought to live holy and godly lives' (2 Peter 3:11). And Paul encourages Titus to 'set ... an example by doing what is good', and slaves 'to show that they can be fully trusted, so that in every way they will make the teaching about God our Saviour attractive' (Titus 2:7, 10).

That's what our belief should produce in us!

Notes

1 John Stott, *The Cross of Christ* (IVP, 1986), p. 203.
2 John Stott, *Christ the Controversialist* (Tyndale Press, 1970), p. 26.

GOD AND HIS WORD

CHAPTER ONE

Sometimes people think of the UCCF Doctrinal Basis only in terms of its eleven clauses (a) to (k). But the introductory sentence puts them all in proper perspective. It reads: 'The doctrinal basis of the Fellowship shall be the fundamental truths of Christianity, as revealed in Holy Scripture, including . . .'. This reminds us that the Bible itself is the source of all the truths contained in the subsequent statements, and these points are essential to the gospel itself. This chapter looks briefly at the first three clauses, which speak of God and his Word.

The Holy Trinity

The unity of the Father, the Son and the Holy Spirit in the Godhead.

When we begin to think about God's person and character we soon realize that he is too vast for our finite minds to grasp. Perhaps nothing makes us feel more intellectually helpless than the teaching about the three Persons in the one Godhead. The early disciples of our Lord were Jews and therefore strict monotheists (*i.e.* they believed in one God, Deuteronomy 6:4). And yet without in any way abandoning their faith in the Old Testament they did not hesitate to acknowledge that Jesus was God the Son. Then Jesus himself promised that he would send his disciples 'another Counsellor', whom he also called 'the Spirit of truth' (John 14:16, 17). As Jesus taught more about the Person and work of the Holy Spirit, and as the early disciples experienced more of him, the 'tri-unity' in the Godhead became clear.

It has been said that we get confused because we think of God as mathematically 'one', as distinct from three. It is more helpful to see him as 'God alone' (Deuteronomy 6:4), as distinct from idols.

The basic scriptural revelation is unmistakably clear that there is only one true God. But even in the Old Testament we find hints of a depth and complexity in the one true God. For example, the common name for God, *Elohim*, is plural in form (see Genesis 1:26–27, 3:22) and points to 'the fulness of life and of power which are present in God'.[1] God is also said to create by his word (Psalm 33:6, and by his Spirit (Genesis 1:2).

After God had spoken through his Son in New Testament days, the church saw and taught that Jesus was God, and yet distinct from the Father; that the Holy Spirit was God and yet distinct from both the Father and the Son. The Godhead is one, but complex. The Father is not the Son. The Son is not the Holy Spirit. But the Father, the Son and the Spirit are equally God. If we note how the Bible refers to Father, Son and Holy Spirit, we see their distinctness coming across in many ways. (See Matthew 16:15–17; 28:19; John 14:16; 16:7–15; 20:24–31; 2 Corinthians 13:14; Ephesians 2:18; 1 Peter 1:2; Revelation 1:4–5.) Yet, as the Creeds express it, they are one in 'substance' or 'essence'.

Perhaps it's a blow to our pride to find something that we really can't understand. But it shouldn't surprise us when we are facing the infinite God, and we should be a little wary of illustrations that are supposed to help us to understand the Trinity. If we reach the point of thinking we *understand* it, we may be sure that we have gone wrong somewhere! We should rather respond to what we can't understand in humble praise.

God has made us 'social' beings, needing one another's company. There is something very wonderful about the fact that in this we are made in the image of a God who is in some mysterious way a 'community' of three in himself. He is not absolutely solitary. He understands our desire for fellowship. He is like that himself.

Some of the puzzling features of the Bible's teaching about the relationship of the three Persons of the Trinity to one another are solved when we realize that we are taught two different aspects of this. The first relates to God's essential nature, or 'essence'. The second relates more to the work done by the different members of the Trinity in the work of Salvation. Both sides of this contain things which are beyond us, and we are always inclined to think of God too much as a single Person or as three Gods! It is wonderful to remember that the New Testament brings these truths to us not as philosophical propositions but as a picture of the God of grace who has saved us and made us his own. We may not be able to see the whole picture, but it is the picture of a God who has shown us his grace and love in creation and redemption, to whom the believer responds in praise and adoration.

Putting this clause at the beginning of the Doctrinal Basis reminds us that the supreme purpose of all our being is to know and serve the one supreme God. A true view of the character of God is the foundation of all theology (Isaiah 6:3; John 4:24; 1 Timothy 1:17).

Sovereignty

The sovereignty of God in creation, revelation, redemption and final judgment.

Twentieth-century people, and sometimes even twentieth-century Christians, often have an inadequate picture of God. We so easily make ourselves and the measure of our thoughts the standard by which we judge everything else. But the Bible shows us a God who can't be measured in human terms (see Isaiah 40:18–20, 25–26). He is the beginning and the end of everything (Revelation 1:8). Only if we acknowledge that can we get our bearings and come to a true understanding of ourselves. He is the first and final cause of all that is (Romans 11:36). He reigns supreme (Psalm 115:3; Romans 9:5; 1 Corinthians 8:4, 6; Revelation 19:6). Everything that takes place is within his will. He overrules human actions and directs them to his own purposes (Genesis 45:7–8; 50:20; Ephesians 1:11;

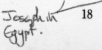
Joseph in Egypt.

18

Revelation 4:11). All things were created by his decision and through his action (Psalm 33:6; Hebrews 11:3). All things are preserved by his power.

When the first man and woman fell into sin, it was God who punished them (see Genesis 3:16–19) and God who planned their salvation (Mark 10:45; Hebrews 1:1–2; 1 John 4:9–10). He revealed his plan of salvation in Christ the Mediator and Saviour, a plan he had made before the foundation of the world (see Ephesians 1:4; 1 Peter 1:20). When he brings us to know him we become aware that that saving work is God's alone and is all 'to the praise of his glorious grace' (Ephesians 1:6). This divine Lord might justly have acted very differently. He chose, however, to be gracious and to bring his saving grace to sinners.

In the same way, we are all in his hands for the future (Romans 2:6–8). All must finally give account to him as Judge (2 Corinthians 5:10), and he will have the last word in settling their eternal destiny (Revelation 20:12–13). No-one can evade him (Hebrew 9:27).

Alongside these truths, the Bible teaches with equal plainness that mankind is morally responsible before God (see Genesis 3:11–13 compared with 3:17; Romans 1:18–20; 3:5–8). There is no hint of fatalism. We cannot excuse ourselves before God. The sovereignty of God and the responsibility of men and women live side by side in the pages of Scripture, although with our limited minds we may not be able to understand how they can be reconciled.

19

The Bible

The divine inspiration and infallibility of Holy Scripture as originally given, and its supreme authority in all matters of faith and conduct.

Christian belief about the Bible is the third item in the Basis. This may seem strange in the light of all we have stressed so far on the place of the Bible. But the order is deliberate. Unless we believe in the God who reveals himself to mankind we will make no sense of the Bible's purpose. What we believe about God will affect what we believe about the Bible.

What we believe about the Bible affects almost everything else of importance. So we must spend some time on it. We'll look at this clause phrase by phrase.

a. 'Holy Scripture'

This refers to the sixty-six books normally found in the Bible, as used by the churches of the Reformation, and listed in the historic confessions. We call this list of included books the 'canon', a word which means, in this context, a rule or standard. There are other books which have sometimes been included (*e.g.* by the Roman Catholic Church), usually called the Apocrypha. These books are not in the same category as the sixty-six and were not recognized by the early church as having the same authority. This is not simply a position which has been held since the sixteenth-century but rests, we believe, on sound historical foundations.

How did this 'canon' develop? Its history is a complex one, and it is probably better to refer to one of the works given in the notes on p. 39 if you would like to learn more. (The articles in the *New Bible Dictionary*[2] are helpful.[3]) But we believe that in accepting these sixty-six books we are following Christ. Both Old and New Testaments derive their greatest authority from the Lord Jesus Christ himself.

How can we say that? The Old Testament as we know it – whether in Hebrew or in the Greek translation that was well established by Jesus' time – was his Bible. He obeyed it and lived by it. He taught from it and taught others to obey it. He regarded it as instruction from his heavenly Father. Jesus' Bible was the thirty-nine books of our Old Testament today.

During his life on earth Jesus made teaching and preaching his main task – until he came to die. He chose twelve apostles to continue the teaching task, giving them a very special commission, and equipping them by the Spirit to declare the truth about him with authority. The New Testament is part of their response to this commission. They – or, in some cases, others close to them – put the apostolic teaching down in written form for the benefit of future generations. When the early church came to discuss which books should be accepted as having authority the key question was that of apostolicity: Was a book written either by an apostle, or by men who had been so close to the apostles, that the doctrine they taught was apostolic?

Although the word 'apostle' is used in different ways in the New Testament we can see clearly that the original eleven and Paul carried an authority in laying down the foundation of Christian truth that cannot be equalled or repeated (see Ephesians 2:20; 1 Corinthians 3:9–11). We can also see that the New Testament teaches us not to expect any further revelation before the coming of Christ (using the word 'revelation' to mean communication of authoritative teaching that must be received and obeyed by all). In this sense revelation has ceased. Since his first coming we are in 'the last days' (Hebrews 1:1–2). Having given us the Bible, the Holy Spirit's work now is to help us to understand it, not to add to it. The Bible is sufficient. We need living and powerful exposition and application of the Bible, but not any fresh authoritative teaching. History shows that whenever men add to the Bible they end up taking away from it. They confuse its message or distort its balance.

b. 'Divine inspiration'

There are two questions that we must ask ourselves when we come to think about the inspiration of the Bible. The first is, 'What does the Bible itself teach about its inspiration?' The second is, 'Is that teaching true?'

Let's begin with the first of these. If you read the Bible carefully you can't mistake the fact that it sees itself as something that comes *from* God and not as the result of man struggling to find out about God. The books of the Bible are human books (that is, differing in style and vocabulary), but not just that. God is their ultimate author. He spoke because without that we would not be able to know him. The writer to the Hebrews puts it like this: 'God spoke to our forefathers through the prophets' (Hebrews 1:1).

This means that when we use the word 'inspiration' about the Bible we are using it in a different sense from when we speak about an 'inspired' work of art. When Paul writes to Timothy about the Old Testament in 2 Timothy 3:16 he says (according to many versions) 'all Scripture is inspired by God'. But he uses an unusual Greek word which the NIV translates, more literally, as 'God-breathed' (literally *expired*, 'breathed out'). So the Bible is seen as God's speech. The great phrase of the Old Testament prophets gives us the same idea: 'Thus says the Lord ...'. We have a Bible because God has chosen to speak to us.

The Bible, for the writers of the New Testament, was our Old Testament. How did they see it? They quote it as being the word of God, or what God says, or what the Holy Spirit says. They use phrases like 'God says', or 'the Scriptures say', or 'it says' interchangeably (see, for instance, Genesis 12:3, 8 and Galatians 3:8; also Hebrews 3:7). So the Bible's view of itself might be put like this '... a supernatural, providential influence of God's Holy Spirit upon the human authors which caused them to write what He wished to be written'.[4] (By 'providential', J. I. Packer here means God's overall control of all that happens.)

The Bible's view is that God has spoken to us through the mighty events of history that we read about in the Bible. But the record itself is God's written revelation, his own explanation of and commentary on the history. It not only contains the

Word of God; it also *is* the Word of God. And this does not simply become true when we believe it! It is true all along, but we only begin to grasp this when the Holy Spirit opens our eyes.

Sometimes evangelicals are accused of believing that the human authors of the Bible were mere puppets as they wrote. That is not what we find in the Bible itself. Their writing was a real human process. God used many different authors, from different cultures, writing in different languages, having different personalities, using different literary styles. And in all of that he was in control. Sometimes – but not often – the human author was comparatively passive as he received some revelation directly from God (*e.g.*, see Revelation 1:10–11). But we get the impression that usually God was using each man's personality and active thinking to the full (*e.g.*, see Luke 1:1–4). This brings us to the old problem of God's sovereignty and human freedom. But both of these are taught in the Bible and the same is true of the Bible's own inspiration. *Men* wrote; *God* was in control. Perhaps it helps to compare this with the Lord Jesus Christ himself: he is human; he is also divine.

We live in an age when people often value feelings more than words. But of course we need words even to be able to express feelings properly. Love, for example, is more than words, but words can express much more fully what someone feels about us. So we needn't hesitate to speak of the Bible as 'propositional revelation'. We don't mean that the Bible consists of abstract philosophical statements. But through all its various forms and styles God is using words to tell us what we need to know. Whatever the Bible tells us, in all its variety, is being told us by God himself. God in his fullness is beyond the limits of human language to express or describe, and so is our salvation (see Job 11:7–9; Isaiah 40:12–14; 1 Timothy 6:16; Ephesians 3:19; 1 Corinthians 2:9). But we cannot know properly about God or his grace without the words he has given us in the Bible (see 2 Timothy 3:15).[5]

So much for what the Bible says about itself. That's the right place to start, because in the end we accept the inspiration of the Bible as a matter of faith in just the same way as we accept any other truth in the Bible. But there is more to say, and it's important to turn to the second of our two questions: 'Is the Bible's teaching true?'

It is important to do this because some people accuse us of using a circular argument – quoting from the Bible itself to prove its truth, *i.e.* assuming its reliability in order to prove it! Now there's some truth in that, and in fact there has to be. If the Bible is God's Word there cannot be any higher authority to test it by. No-one else can give us any guarantees on the subject. When we're looking at things that are quite outside the reach of the human mind we have to depend on help from outside ourselves. You can't establish confidence in the Bible by the traditional methods of scientific proofs, for example.

But God does give us other ways of approaching the problem. We can strengthen our confidence in the Bible by a whole complex of interlocking and reinforcing arguments. We trust in a God who wishes to reveal himself and not to leave us in the dark. We learn to know the Lord Jesus Christ and cannot doubt him or his teaching. But we can also look at a range of outside evidence which doesn't for the most part *prove* the Bible but which adds weight to the whole argument.

The Bible claims to deal with historical events. Many of the events it records relate to people and periods which appear in other ancient records. An enormous amount of additional information of this sort has been uncovered in the last hundred years, confirming the Bible's reliability in an amazing number of ways. As a result many of the earlier sceptical criticisms of the Bible's historical accuracy have been demolished.

Then let's look at the evidence of what the Bible's effect has been in human society. Nations and communities which have come under its influence have been transformed. Evil has been restrained; compassion has been generated; family and other social structures have been stabilized; self-discipline has been restored. The Bible apparently isn't just a book of sterile ideas: it changes people! And we Christians know that that is true of us: we have come to know God in Christ through the truth of the Bible, and have experienced changes which nothing else could have produced. It has brought us light and life; its teaching has brought us to a new experience of God; it has transforming power. How could it be merely a collection of human ideas?

Finally, if we drop this view of the Bible we very seriously affect our view of Christ's authority.[6] If Jesus was wrong in what he said about the Old Testament, who is to say he was right anywhere? But if Jesus is our Lord we must believe him and follow him here as much as on other points like the forgiveness of sins and his teaching on heaven and hell.

So we have a web of mutually reinforcing arguments: we believe in a God who wants us to know him; the Holy Spirit persuades us of the Lordship of Christ and the trustworthiness of the Bible; outside sources give us abundant confirmation of whatever they touch on; we see clearly the good faith of the writers and the transforming effect of their writings on human lives; we too have been transformed by the message!

What room is there left for doubt?

c. 'Infallibility'

This word is important but often misunderstood. It means something which cannot mislead, and so is entirely trustworthy. It's a word that has been used about the Bible for a very long time: Wycliffe, in the fourteenth-century, spoke of the Bible as 'the infallible rule of truth', and the same idea has found expression since. The Westminster Confession, for example, speaks of 'the infallible truth and divine authority of the Bible'. But by now the idea shouldn't surprise us. What we have been learning so far about the inspiration of the Bible should have prepared us for this thought. The Bible tells us about a God who is infallible. As the ultimate author of Scripture he has infallibly revealed himself. So Scripture will be infallible. It is a word that tells us that God's saving message is true and reliable. It is a word that gives us confidence in a wavering and uncertain world. Augustine's phrase for it was: 'What Scripture says, God says'; the Bible is the infallible God speaking infallibly to us.

But the word has a bad press in many people's eyes. Sometimes this is because they genuinely reject what we mean by it, but there are also a lot of misunderstandings around. Let's look at some of these.

It shouldn't be necessary to say so, but of course we don't mean that false statements which are simply recorded by the Bible are true (for example the false arguments used by the Pharisees). Common sense will usually be enough for us to see what the author of the book really wants us to accept.

Infallibility doesn't mean a literalistic approach, either. We don't defend imposing a mechanical or unnatural meaning on the text. 'History must be treated as history, poetry as poetry, hyperbole and metaphor as hyperbole and metaphor, generalization and approximation as what they are, and so forth. . . . The truthfulness of Scripture is not negated by the appearance in it of irregularities of grammar or spelling, phenomenal descriptions [*i.e.* descriptions according to how things *appear*] of nature, reports of false statements (*e.g.* the lies of Satan), or seeming discrepancies between one passage and another.'[7] The Bible describes events and phenomena, whether historical, natural or supernatural, with the language and terminology appropriate to the authors' times and culture, but their descriptions are trustworthy. They need to be correctly understood.

We must be on our guard here against any temptation to treat religious truth differently from historical claims. God revealed himself in history and some of the historical events of the Bible are absolutely fundamental to the Christian faith. We can't separate the saving message from the historical context: if one goes, so does the other. Doctrine and history, event and interpretation, belong together. Christ often referred to Old Testament events, as well as to Old Testament teaching, and sometimes the whole point of what he was saying depended on their historicity (see Matthew 12:41; Luke 11:50–51).[8]

Even where the events he referred to are not fundamental to our salvation we can't doubt them ourselves without casting doubts on the one who said that 'the Scripture cannot be broken' (John 10:35).

But doesn't the rise of modern science make it difficult to accept the Bible's accounts of supernatural events? Not at all. Of course we must recognize that the Bible doesn't use scientific terms or concepts. It doesn't tell us about the 'laws' of nature. Instead it tells us other things, for instance that all the universe is under God's control, that all its phenomena, ordinary and extraordinary, regular and miraculous, recurring and unique, are expressions of his activity. Scripture and nature both speak of the one true God so can't be in real conflict. Of course they will seem to be if we misunderstand what one of them is saying. Science is concerned to understand how natural phenomena relate to one another; Scripture, on the whole, is more concerned with how they relate to God.

Science in general asks *how*, and Scripture in general explains *why*. So natural science and biblical theology are really complementary.

When biblical writers speak about the things that science also touches on, we believe that they speak reliably although they use the popular and pre-scientific language of their own time. What else could they have done, without failing to be the word of God to all the generations of God's people who have lived since? Old Testament cosmological language pictures heaven as literally above the sky (the firmament) and Sheol (Hades, the place of the dead) as literally below the ground, and it has a physiological way of describing psychological experience – bones speaking, bowels yearning, kidneys instructing.

J. I. Packer says:

> It may be doubted whether these forms of speech were any more 'scientific' in character and intent than modern references to the sun rising, or light-headedness, or walking on air, or one's heart sinking into one's boots, would be. It is much likelier that they were simply standard pieces of imagery, which the writers utilized, and sometimes heightened for poetic effect, without a thought of what they would imply for cosmology and physiology if taken literally. And language means no more than it is used to mean.[9]

Some interpreters seem to think that the biblical writers used language in a wooden and almost unhuman way. They try to make the writers teach things which don't seem to have been any part of what they were meaning to say. And that is what we always want to know: what does the passage intend to say? what does it mean? why was it written? This doesn't often have a large scientific content though it may often include matters of fact and history. And the Bible describes these *in its own idiom* (*e.g.* population numbers are often rounded up or down to the nearest thousand).

Using technical terms in controversial areas is hazardous. Sometimes people continue to use them while meaning something quite different from previously accepted usage. This has happened in this area, too, as Packer records:

> Verbal currency, as we know, can be devalued. Any word may have some of its meaning rubbed off, and this has happened to all my preferred terms for stating my belief about the Bible. I hear folk declare Scripture *inspired* and in the next breath say that it misleads from time to time. I hear them call it *infallible* and *authoritative*, and find they mean only that its impact on us and the commitment to which it leads us will keep us in God's grace, not that it is all true.[10]

But in the Doctrinal Basis our word 'infallible' means that high view of Scripture that has traditionally been meant by it. It is entirely trustworthy in all it affirms, and that includes matters of science and history. As Francis Schaeffer once said: 'It is entirely trustworthy in all of which it speaks – and it speaks of everything!'

There is a great difference between the trustworthiness of the Bible itself and the accuracy of our interpretations of it! We might have a high view of the Bible's authority but still be muddled in our understanding of its meaning. We may believe in its infallibility but that doesn't make the task of interpreting it magically easy. It is the meaning of Scripture, strictly speaking, that is infallible, and to discover that meaning with exactness often requires devout and scholarly work. We have no right to twist or allegorize texts, or to impose fanciful meanings on them. It is very easy to read *into* the text ideas of our own which cannot be fairly read *out* of it! Of course, we need spiritual discernment to understand the Bible (*e.g.* see 1 Corinthians 2) and with that an uneducated seeker after God may often come straight to the meaning while an expert in linguistic or historical research may stumble over the obvious. But there is no place here for laziness! The history of the church shows that belief in the Bible's infallibility has been one of the greatest stimuli to fruitful thinking.

The Bible isn't a collection of proof-texts that we can apply mechanically to every situation and problem. That is not how God chooses to deal with us, although sometimes we might prefer it! The variety of ways God has used to speak to us in the Bible means that we have to apply our fallible minds to understand what he has said to us. We are not merely machines decoding a computer program into typed instructions. In the Bible God speaks to his children. We must respond as children to his infallible and authoritative voice as soon as we understand what he is saying. But like children we do not always get it right. That is our fault, not his.

We do not always listen carefully enough or think over what we have heard before we act.

Christians in every age are tempted to be lazy, intellectually as well as in other ways. But God calls us to worship him with our minds as well as our hearts, and the Bible is a book that addresses our minds. Our first task should be to find out, carefully and accurately, what God is saying to us and our generation in his infallible word.

d. 'As originally given'

We no longer have the original manuscripts of the biblical books. So why should we apply our statement of the Bible's inspiration to the originals and not in the same way to copies and translations? Isn't that just some kind of evasion of a difficulty? Not at all! These words have a positive and legitimate purpose and are an important part of our statement of the doctrine of Scripture. Why?

It is part of normal literary source-studies to distinguish between the author's original manuscript and subsequent revisions or editions. To this day literary scholars will discuss the status of different versions even of, say, nineteenth-century works, trying to discern author-amendments from editorial amendments, *etc*. What is supremely important is what the *author* wished to say. So the idea is not confined to biblical studies.

Then this phrase reminds us of the fallibility of transcription and translation processes. Though the Greek and Hebrew texts are amazingly well preserved, God has not undertaken to prevent the slips and inaccuracies which crept into the work of copyists and translators. We still need scientific textual criticism to determine the wording of the inspired original as best we can. Biblical scholars have in fact an astonishing wealth of material on which to work – more than for any other ancient document. And by now we can be confident of a text (especially for the New Testament) that must be identical with the originals in all but comparatively insignificant details.

But perhaps the most important reason for relating our statement of infallibility to the original documents is that the Bible's clearest and strongest statements about its inspiration appear to do this (*e.g.* see 2 Timothy 3:16 and 2 Peter 1:21). God has wonderfully preserved the truths of the Bible through transmission and translation processes, but the highest claims for its trustworthiness refer to men who 'spoke from God as they were carried along by the Holy Spirit' (2 Peter 1:21).

Sometimes people find difficulty in the way New Testament writers occasionally quote freely from the Old Testament. But if they remain faithful to the thought of the passage they quote (*e.g.* see Ephesians 4:8; Hebrews 10:5–7), we surely have no problem. All translators paraphrase the originals, more or less. In fact, many of these quotations are of the 'pesher' type, combining quotation with interpretation – a type of quotation which was as common among the Jews as it is today in Christian sermons, and which appears equally legitimate in both cases.[11]

What of the objection that some of the books of the Old Testament are thought to be composite works, some of multiple authorship, some where an original version may already have been augmented or edited before it reached the status of canonical Scripture? Does this make it invalid to refer to documents 'as originally given'? Not at all. It may be impossible for us to unravel the development of some books, but the clear statement of Scripture is that there was a revelatory process, and that the completed books are infallible.

But finally, where does that leave me, today, with the Bible I have in my hand? How does it help me to accept as infallible a document I no longer have? Remember first that we can have every confidence that our modern Bibles very closely reflect the content and meaning of the originals. Thousands of textual variants of the New Testament are known, and none which bear scholarly scrutiny affect any major point of Christian doctrine.

Then, if we have confidence in a God who wishes to reveal himself we can be sure that he will not allow the light of that revelation to be quenched. We also have the encouragement of the examples of the New Testament authors. They, too, depended on copies of the Old Testament, and in fact in many cases they used a Greek translation and not the original Hebrew. Yet they still show implicit trust in it. They were as aware of the difficulties as we are, but they give us a practical example of how to make use of the Bible we have. So we, too, are safe in submitting to it, never questioning or deviating from the smallest part without good textual evidence.

e. 'Supreme authority'

Authority – that is, the right to rule us – belongs to God, and God's authority is expressed in and through the Bible. Reason, religious experience and church tradition all have their place in helping us to understand it, but none of them may be set above it. In fact, Scripture must be allowed to judge all three and to correct them where necessary.

We sometimes hear people say that to bow to the supreme authority of Holy Scripture is bibliolatry. But that is not so. We don't worship a book, but we do accept the authority of the book as a basic part of our worship of God because it is God's Word. To reject its authority would be to reject God's authority. Psalm 119 wonderfully expresses what the Christian's attitude should be to God's will conveyed through his Word.

Where does church tradition fit in, then? Jesus' life and teaching shed light on this. He distinguished 'the word of God' (commands of Scripture) from the rabbinic 'traditions of men', denying that the latter had final authority (Mark 7:6ff., 13). He went on to commission his own apostles to lay down authoritative teaching, too, and the tradition of the apostles – that is, their transmitted teaching – is part of the Word of God, binding on Christians at all times (cf. 2 Thessalonians 2:15; 3:6).

Traditions or spiritual insights of later ages are not a second source of divine teaching to supplement Scripture, but are only a series of attempts (valuable but not always successful) to interpret and express biblical faith. In every case the Bible itself must judge these attempts.

Can we take the Bible to be essentially clear, self-interpreting, and able to speak for itself? Not all that it teaches is equally easily understood, but it will give us the truth that we need to be saved and to be godly, through the illumination given by the Holy Spirit who inspired it. And the Bible is sufficient: no further infallible teaching is needed for us to know God or to serve him.

So when we come to try to understand the Bible we need to be teachable and receptive. We need to search out each writer's intended meaning and bring it to bear upon modern life. Scripture must expose and correct our own presuppositions, and progressively bring our thinking into line with its own. As a matter of conscience, we must trust the biblical promises, obey the biblical commands, and bring our questions to the Bible for answers.

We need God's grace to cultivate humility, to make us open to new insights into biblical truth, responsive to his will, and dependent on the Spirit of God. We may find it helpful to pray that God would help us understand, remember, love, obey and then transmit what we learn from Scripture. If we do this we will discover in our own lives that 'All Scripture is God-breathed and is useful for teaching, rebuking, correcting and training in righteousness, so that the man of God may be thoroughly equipped for every good work' (2 Timothy 3:16–17).

f. 'In all matters of faith and conduct'

Faith and behaviour belong together. Without biblical truth we can't maintain the Christian life for long. As 2 Timothy 3:16–17 reminds us, biblical teaching is for both life and thought. If we allow our discussion of Christianity to stop at a theoretical level we are unbiblical. And as the pattern of most of the New Testament letters shows, doctrine is worked out in application, in worship and in evangelism. It is because God is as he is and man is in the state he is that Paul can write: 'Therefore, I urge you, brothers, in view of God's mercy, to offer your bodies as living sacrifices, holy and pleasing to God' (Romans 12:1).

We believe that the UCCF Doctrinal Basis is biblical in emphasizing the doctrinal foundation of Christianity on which all else is built. It does not attempt a summary of details of Christian practice: the New Testament shows that such attempts easily become distorted into legalism, but it has no hesitation about summaries of doctrine.

We have looked at the *affirmations* of the first three clauses of the doctrinal basis. What *denials* do they imply? Man is *not* independent or self-sufficient, morally or intellectually. The universe is *not* a purposeless mechanism, and human society, in this technological age, is lawless and degenerate. It has *not* shaken itself free from God's control. We are *not* helpless, at the mercy of mindless historical, biological or sociological forces. Man's mind is darkened and is *not* sufficient for the task of solving life's great mysteries. But we are *not* left without the light we need to know God, and to face the ethical and moral decisions that we face in this confused world. The Bible is *not* just a collection of ancient human writings. It is *not* full of errors, reflecting the fallibility of the men who wrote it.

God is not weak! He is not silent!

Notes

1 H. Bavinck, *Our Reasonable Faith*, translated by H. Zylstra (Baker Book House, Grand Rapids, 1977), p. 147.

2 *New Bible Dictionary* (IVP, second edition 1982). See the articles 'Bible' by F. F. Bruce (pp. 137–140), 'Canon of the Old Testament' by R. T. Beckwith (pp. 166–171), and 'Canon of the New Testament' by J. N. Birdsall (pp. 171–177).

3 For a more thorough discussion, see David G. Dunbar, 'The Biblical Canon', in D. A. Carson and John D. Woodbridge (eds.), *Hermeneutics, Authority and Canon* (IVP, 1986).

4 J. I. Packer, *'Fundamentalism' and the Word of God* (IVF, 1958), p. 77.

5 For a detailed discussion, see Wayne A. Grudem, 'Scripture's Self-attestation', in D. A. Carson and John D. Woodbridge (eds.), *Scripture and Truth* (IVP, 1983).

6 See J. W. Wenham, *Christ and the Bible* (Tyndale Press, 1972).

7 From 'The Chicago Statement on Biblical Inerrancy (1978)'; quoted in Packer, *God Has Spoken* (Hodder, 1979), pp. 152–153.

8 See J. W. Wenham, *Christ and the Bible* (Tyndale Press, 1972).

9 J. I. Packer, *'Fundamentalism' and the Word of God* (IVF, 1958), p. 97, note 2.

10 J. I. Packer, *Freedom, Authority and Scripture* (IVP, 1982), p. 56.

11 See E. E. Ellis, *Paul's Use of the Old Testament* (Baker Book House, 1957); and M. Silva, 'The New Testament Use of the Old Testament: text form and authority' in D. A. Carson and John D. Woodbridge (eds.), *Scripture and Truth* (IVP, 1983).

MANKIND AND REDEMPTION

Earlier in this century, people were very optimistic about human nature. Even today, after all that we can see of human wickedness, some men and women still try to hold on to a belief in mankind's basic goodness. But as they look at human history during the past few decades many thinkers have come to their wits' end in trying to unravel the mystery of life. A cosy belief in human goodness looks rather threadbare today. Perhaps people will be readier to hear what God has to say on the subject.

The more we see of God, the more mankind's darkness stands out by contrast. We have already seen that God has not stood by helplessly in the face of our human plight. He has spoken, and for a reason. He has told us about himself. And he has acted to save us. The four clauses covered in this chapter tell us more about mankind's condition and God's remedy.

41

The fall of man

The universal sinfulness and guilt of human nature since the fall, rendering man subject to God's wrath and condemnation.

The Bible presents the fall of man as an historical event. Genesis 1 and 2 describe God creating man and the rest of the universe as perfect. 'God saw all that he had made, and it was very good.' Then Genesis 3 describes (i) man as a creation of God and as responsible to him, (ii) God giving a clear word of guidance to man about the conduct of his life and (iii) a deliberate act of disobedience to this divine word. The New Testament writers accept the fact of this act of rebellion and build upon it as they explain the Christian gospel (Romans 5:12–21, 1 Corinthians 15:21–22).

Many other explanations for human wickedness and misery have been offered. But non-Christian thought falls down most often at the point where it rejects what the Bible teaches about human nature. What we find in Genesis is not just a pictorial representation of some general 'tribal' or racial wrongdoing. Nor is the fall of mankind a mere incident on our upward movement to moral consciousness. Genesis 3 describes a disastrous *downward* step from the perfection of chapters 1 and 2. There is no place in the Bible for ideas of a gradual development of moral sense. It clearly teaches that our moral nature was deeply affected when our first parents rebelled. Only the biblical account adequately explains the tendency we see in all men and women to sin, and our universal experience of guilt (Genesis 3; Romans 1:18 – 3:20; 5:12–21).

So by an act of deliberate choice the first man and woman rebelled against God's commands and became God's enemies. As a result they lost that fellowship with their creator which they had enjoyed. And the whole of the human race, proceeding from Adam as its ancestor, has become morally degenerate. Every part of the personality of every person is affected by this degeneracy. That is what theologians mean by 'total depravity': not that all men are as evil as they could be but that the effects of sin reach into every part of our make-up. It has darkened our minds, distorted our emotions and enslaved our wills. Left to ourselves we cannot possibly get back to the original condition of moral and spiritual harmony with God.

But we are still moral beings, judging actions according to some standard of right and wrong. We still recognize that we are obliged to do good, even when we find that we cannot do it in practice. We know something of the law of our Maker, either by nature through conscience or by special revelation in the Bible. And we know that we must obey it.

God's laws are good. In them he tells us what he demands of us and what is good for us. It was the devil's suggestion that God's demands were unreasonable and unjust that led mankind into sin in the first place, and continues to do so (see 1 John 3:4). So we may not separate off and evade those commandments we find inconvenient. If we do we defy the Lawgiver and bring God's judgment on our heads. We also often bring disastrous consequences in this life upon ourselves, our family, or on society.

Today we use the word 'guilt' in various ways
which often overlook the basic biblical idea of guilt.
This refers not to our feelings but to our relationship with God. To be guilty is to be under a legal
sentence, whatever we may *feel* about it. When the
Holy Spirit opens a person's eyes to his condition he
begins to feel guilty and ashamed, but he was
actually guilty before he realized it (see Psalm
51:1–4). He was under God's just condemnation.

Both the Old and New Testaments speak quite
clearly about God's anger at sin (see Genesis 6:5–7;
Psalm 95:10–11; Romans 1:18; 2:8–9). That is not
popular language today. This is partly because our
society is often confused on the nature of law and
guilt, and partly because we always try to excuse
ourselves and minimize our guilt. Fashions of
thought in psychology have made this worse by
diverting the blame for many things from us to our
past or present environment. But evasion of guilt is
as old as Adam! (See Genesis 3:12.) The Bible constantly refers to what theologians term God's
judicial displeasure against sin.

Let's not misunderstand this. For us anger
usually means something uncontrolled, selfish and
ugly, and we find it difficult to think about a sinless
God being angry. But God's anger is pure and perfect: it reflects his passionate commitment to what
is right, and the world would be a dark place if our
God were not like that. Sometimes we hear people
trying to soften this by saying that 'God hates the
sin but loves the sinner'. But that can be mis-
leading. It is not true if it implies that God has no
response of anger and condemnation against the

44

sinner himself (see Ephesians 2:3). God's anger is not just something directed against sin as something impersonal. As the creator he still loves men and women, but we must face the fact that we are sinners and God is displeased with us.

In this sense wrath is as permanent a feature of God's character as love (see Romans 11:22). It is the reaction of holiness to unrighteousness. Because God is perfectly righteous, fallen mankind – unrepentant and unredeemed – must be the object of his just condemnation. And if we undervalue the Bible's teaching on God's wrath we also fail to grasp the depth of his love (Ephesians 2:3–5). Even more, we will misunderstand the meaning of the death of Christ (Romans 3:22–26).

So we are all by nature at enmity with God, we have an inbuilt bias to sin, and we break what we know to be God's law.

The Saviour

The full deity of the Lord Jesus Christ, the incarnate Son of God; his virgin birth and his real and sinless humanity; his death on the cross, his bodily resurrection and his present reign in heaven and earth.

Both in its teaching and in its worship the Christian church has always struggled to find the right words in speaking about the Lord Jesus Christ. Clear thinking expressed in clear words has been necessary in order to defend the faith against error. This is to be seen in the way in which the New Testament speaks of 'the faith' and 'the truth' – terms which

45

indicate that the gospel has a definable content (see 2 Timothy 4:7 and Jude 3 for 'the faith'; Galatians 2:5 and 1 Timothy 3:15–16 for 'the truth').

No subject in the Bible is more important than its teaching on the person and work of Jesus Christ. If we go wrong here, we go wrong on almost everything else. That is not surprising because not only is the Bible the revelation from God but Christ is himself the revelation that God has given. 'God . . . has spoken . . . by his Son' (Hebrews 1:2).

Jesus came into the world in a supernatural way, and his physical departure from it was also supernatural. The miraculous conception and virgin birth of Jesus, and his miraculous resurrection and ascension are plainly recorded facts. The New Testament bears witness to them all as being real historical events (Matthew 1:18–23; Luke 1:26–31; 1 Corinthians 15:1–8; Acts 1:9; *cf.* 1 Timothy 3:16).

Jesus Christ was, and is, the eternal Son of God, who was conceived by the Holy Spirit and born of the Virgin Mary. He was, and is, true and perfect Man and perfect God. He combines two natures in one Person.

a. 'Full deity'

People have often tried to argue that Jesus Christ is somehow different from us, while denying that he is fully God. Some have suggested that he was the greatest of created beings. Some that he was a man more closely in tune with God than other people. And some again that he was simply more filled with the Holy Spirit than the rest of us manage to be. But the Bible teaches very clearly that he was fully

God, and was so from all eternity (John 1:1–2, 14; Galatians 4:4–5; 1 John 4:9–10). It is because this is so astonishing, and because there have been so many subtle attempts to dilute it, that we use this emphatic expression, speaking of his 'full deity'. He shares the very nature of God and has always done so, in a way that is not and can never be true of us or of any other created being.

b. 'The incarnate Son of God'

These words stress that he 'became flesh', which is what 'incarnate' means. They imply that he existed before he was born in Bethlehem. We 'begin' when our earthly life begins, but he has always existed and the Bible speaks of his birth as a 'coming' into the world (*e.g.* 1 Timothy 1:15). He came as a full human being, that we might 'see the Father' (*cf.* John 14:9). He did not abandon or dilute his deity when he became man, though he temporarily laid aside much of its expression. In becoming fully man he did not become less than God.

c. 'His virgin birth and his real and sinless humanity'

Both Matthew and Luke teach clearly and definitely that his was a virgin birth, that his conception was without the intervention of a human father (Matthew 1:18, 20, 23; Luke 1:34–35). But he was no less human for that. He was really and fully man, physically and psychologically. He underwent the normal psychological and physical processes of growth and development (Luke 2:40, 52), and his knowledge in some areas was incomplete (*e.g.*, see

Mark 13:32; *cf.* 11:12–13). He felt hunger (Matthew 4:2; Mark 11:12), he slept (Mark 4:38), he grew weary (John 4:6), he valued human companionship (Mark 14:33). It is easy for us, with our sinful human natures, to assume that, if he was fully human, he must have been a sinner, too. But, although he was tempted as we are (Matthew 4:1–11), he was blameless and perfect (2 Corinthians 5:21; Hebrews 7:26; 1 John 3:5). His enemies could find no fault in him (John 8:46). There was no failure, and no giving in to temptation to sinful thought, word or action.

d. 'His death on the cross and his bodily resurrection'

In many ways the death of the Son of God on the cross will always be beyond the reach of our minds, but the New Testament writers make it clear that he died. His death was no illusion. It was real, physical, ugly and painful. And the one who died was still God incarnate.

The closing sections of each of the Gospels plainly teach that the crucified body of our Lord was raised from the tomb (Romans 1:18 – 3:20; 5:12–21). This claim, together with the facts concerning the death of Christ, became the central part of the witness of the apostles in the early days of the Christian church (Acts 2:23–24; 4:10–12; 10:39–43). By his death on the cross he completed his role as the sacrifice for our sins, and by his resurrection he authenticated it.

The resurrection is an integral part of God's saving work. Easter morning is the complement of

Good Friday and it symbolizes the victory of Christ. Christians are saved by his death and resurrection; they are united to him in them both. In raising Christ from the dead God set his seal of approval on the sacrifice of Calvary, and vindicated Jesus' claim to be the Son of God (Acts 2:31–32; Romans 1:4).

The resurrection showed that God had accepted Christ's sacrifice, and that he had completed his victory over sin and death. It marks a turning-point in the history of God's people. Christ ascended into heaven and there he acts on behalf of his people as their 'Priest' and 'Advocate' before God. And as a result of his resurrection and his ascension, he poured out his Holy Spirit upon the church (Acts 2:33–34, 38–39) to be the Lord the Life-giver, 'the Comforter', and the guide of his disciples in their pilgrimage through this world. They are invited to benefit from and to enter into the 'power of his resurrection' (1 Corinthians 15:12–22).

When Jesus died, the veil of the temple, which separated the worshippers from the inner sanctuary, was miraculously torn. This was to show that the way into the 'holiest' was now open to those who are in Christ. The empty tomb revealed that death had no further dominion over him. He could say to the dying thief, 'Today you will be with me in paradise' (Luke 23:43). His resurrection and ascension completed his victory over death and have opened the way into God's presence for his people (see Ephesians 4:8–13; Hebrews 2:14–18; 4:14–16; 10:19–25).

The New Testament teaches that his resurrection body was in some way very different from his body before his death (although we are not given all the details). It derived from his previous body, but was changed. It was free from some of the limitations of our present bodies. In 1 Corinthians 15:35 the evidence points to the fact that there was a resurrection of the physical body and not simply a survival of the disembodied spirit. It was the body which had been buried which was raised, though in a changed form, adapted to new spiritual conditions. There was both continuity and dissimilarity. More we do not know, but in the life to come the bodies of all his people will be similar to his resurrection body in some ways (Philippians 3:21).✓

e. 'His present reign in heaven and earth'

The great confession of the early church was 'Jesus is Lord' (Romans 10:9). After his humble and obscure earthly ministry he was given a heavenly role – the exercise of power and authority over the whole of creation (*cf.* Philippians 2:5–11 and 1 Corinthians 15; also Ephesians 1). The gateway to this position of triumph was the ascension, which was not just an appropriate end to his time on earth. He is still active on behalf of his people. He is 'head over everything for the church' (Ephesians 1:22). In due course his kingly power will be made visible to all mankind, but it is already a reality (1 Corinthians 15:23–25).✓

Before Jesus returned to heaven he sent his disciples out into all the world, on the foundation that he had all authority in heaven and earth (Matthew 28:18). That gives us confidence as we respond to that call. The whole world is his and he is entitled to send us out to its farthest corners. He rules over all, so we need fear nothing as we go.

In the New Testament there is a tension between two emphases. Jesus Christ *has* all power and authority 'in heaven and on earth' (Matthew 28:18). But the power of the forces of darkness has not yet been entirely liquidated, and they still wage war against God. There is still a great deal of suffering and conflict, even for God's people, in this world. We would be foolish to deny it, or to pretend that Christians can be spared all the sufferings of this life.

When sufferings come, they are under his powerful control and cannot separate us from his love (Romans 8:38–39). When they come, they are used by him for our good, to strengthen and deepen our faith (Romans 5:3–5; 8:28; James 1:2–3). And come they will. Jesus warned of it, and it was part of Paul's essential teaching to newly planted churches (Acts 14:22). Sometimes as Christian students we may feel that our own college or university Union is living proof of the reign of evil. That is the devil's deception. We should take heart as we reflect on the teaching of Scripture: God is on the throne!

> Rejoice, the Lord is King! . . .
> His kingdom cannot fail,
> He rules o'er earth and heaven . . .
> (Charles Wesley)

The Atonement

Redemption from the guilt, penalty and power of sin only through the sacrificial death once and for all time of our representative and substitute, Jesus Christ, the only mediator between God and man.

The death of Christ is at the heart of the whole Christian message. The crucial question which we all must face is: 'Why did Jesus Christ, the Son of God, die?' Christian theology's deepest mystery and most profound truth lie in the answer to this. And just as the Bible's teaching about who Jesus is has been under attack, so has its teaching about what he did, and why.

Was Jesus simply the greatest in a long line of prophets or ethical philosophers? Then it might not be surprising for him to be killed by a nation with such a record of cruel treatment of its spiritual leaders. If he were only a man, perhaps he hoped by his martyrdom to shame sinful humanity into doing the will of God by the 'moral influence' of his example. But the New Testament claims him to be more than a man and a prophet. And the moment we admit that Jesus Christ is God, we have to face the fact that theories like those are futile.

There are always some theologians who dislike the Bible's teaching about sacrifice and react against the sacrificial language of the New Testament. Others seem to want to avoid saying that Christ's death was either 'on our behalf' or 'in our place'. Most modern 'theories' of the atonement don't do justice to these wonderful facts: God the

Son came into the world in order eventually to go to Jerusalem (Luke 9:51) and deliberately to give his life a 'ransom for many' (Mark 10:45; 1 Timothy 2:6; 1 Peter 2:24). As we look at the Bible's accounts we need an explanation which recognizes that Christ had to come into the world to die for the sins of mankind and to reconcile us to God.

All of the benefits of the Christian gospel flow through Christ, and all flow through his death. The Bible tells us about a salvation that is rich, and reaches to all of the effects of the fall. Our guilt is dealt with, and its penalty, by God forgiving us and delivering us from the coming judgment. Our slavery to sin and its power is dealt with, and we are able to 'live a new life' (Romans 6:14, 4). Our subjection to sickness, suffering and death are dealt with, in the promise of the final perfection of his kingdom. Some of these benefits are immediate and complete, but our spiritual and physical perfection are still to come, in the next life.

a. 'Sacrificial death'

The most important aspects of Christ's saving work are that he died as our *Representative* and that he died as our *Substitute*. What do these two words tell us? They are so close, biblically, that the difference in their meaning is not immediately obvious. But they *are* different.

i. Representative. This word stresses that Christ acts on our behalf, by closely identifying with us. It tells us that he acts in our interest, and does things for us that we could not do for ourselves. We think

53

of the examples of a country's ambassador, who represents us and acts on our behalf, or a Member of Parliament. In the case of Jesus, he became man in order to be like me and to save me. And I will share in his blessings. I am a 'co-heir' with Christ (Romans 8:17) and he is my 'brother' (Romans 8:29; Hebrews 2:11).

So I see not only that he does for me what I cannot do for myself, but that he does so by coming near to me, and adopting my cause as his own. Christ is my 'High Priest' (Hebrews 3:1), and the High Priest in the Old Testament was the representative of his people, making sacrifices on their behalf. The idea of the Representative also reminds us of the covenants of the Old Testament, and that reassures me of the certainty of my salvation. God has promised by a covenant to receive those who are Christ's.

Passages which help us to understand this are those which speak of Christ being our 'Adam' (*e.g.* 1 Corinthians 15:45, 47; Romans 5:12ff.). Christ represents the new humanity as Adam represented the old. In this sense our Lord Jesus Christ may be spoken of as the first Representative Man in the new order of mankind, brought into being by his death and resurrection.

In Romans 5, Paul draws out the contrast between the disobedience, sin and death which came through Adam, and the obedience, grace, righteousness and life which came through Christ.

Jesus continues as our Representative, in the presence of God. Paul tells us that we are seated 'with him in the heavenly realms in Christ Jesus'

(Ephesians 2:6). As we are not yet there literally, that must mean that we are there in him as our 'head', our representative. That is meant to assure us of our place there. And John speaks of the ascended Christ as 'one who speaks to the Father in our defence' (1 John 2:1).

ii. Substitute. He became our Representative in order to rescue us. But our plight is that we are under the judgment of God. So in order to save us he had to take our curse, and die in our place. That is what we mean by substitution. He died instead of us. He carried the judgment of God which we deserved. Here the emphasis is not only on our helplessness and our need of someone else to rescue us but on the nature of our problem – guilt and judgment. And that brings us straight to the cross and Christ's death.

We cannot do justice to what we find in the Bible without including the idea of substitution when we try to understand the cross. As John Stott has written, 'Substitution is not "a theory of the atonement" ... It is rather ... the heart of the atonement ... The better people understand the glory of the divine substitution, the easier it will be for them to trust in the Substitute.'[1] Both Jesus and his disciples looked on his death in the light of the illustrations and types which we find in the Old Testament sacrifices. 'The Son of man came ... to give his life as a ransom for many' (Matthew 20:28, RSV). 'This is my blood of the new covenant, which is poured out for many for the forgiveness of sins' (Matthew 26:28).

And as we go on through the New Testament passages referring to Christ's death, we come to see that he died as a vicarious sacrifice (*i.e.* filling the place of another). (See Hebrews 9; Matthew 20:28; 2 Corinthians 5:21; Galatians 2:20; 1 Peter 3:18; Romans 5:10; Philippians 2:8; Hebrews 2:9–14; 1 Corinthians 1:23; Galatians 6:12; Ephesians 2:16. *Cf.* also Leviticus 16; Isaiah 53:4–6.)[2] So Christ offers himself as a sacrifice to God in our place. To do justice to this we need to use words such as 'substitution'.

Heb 9:14

The apostle Peter puts it as follows: 'He himself bore our sins in his body on the tree' (1 Peter 2:24), and 'Christ died for sins once for all, the righteous for the unrighteous, to bring you to God' (1 Peter 3:18). In other words, the apostles taught that the Son of God who came in human form freely chose to suffer the divine judgment that we deserve for our sins. They use very forceful expressions when describing Christ's work, such as 'made . . . sin for us' (2 Corinthians 5:21) and 'becoming a curse for us' (Galatians 3:13).

Perhaps some people find problems with the principle of substitution because they do not reckon sufficiently with the deity of Christ. They talk of substitution as being 'immoral'; and so it would be if it were merely one man's life being substituted for another's. But '*God* was reconciling the world to himself in Christ' (2 Corinthians 5:19), and our human analogies break down at this point.

Then again, people are often unwilling to admit just how radical sin is, and our complete helpless-

56

ness to save ourselves. Human pride rebels at this point, and it is unpalatable to have to acknowledge that we need someone to die in our place.

Christ as our substitute has exhausted the penal consequences of sin in his own person (Isaiah 53:4–6; 1 Peter 1:19). It is not a question of a *quantitative* equivalent, *i.e.* an equal amount of punishment for the totality of human sin. The Bible itself repeatedly focuses attention on the divine *quality* of the sinless Substitute; he met the basic requirements of God's moral government of the world and of his dealings with the root principle of sin.

b. 'The only mediator between God and man'

Our human pride makes it difficult to accept the Bible's teaching of man's utter dependence on God's free grace for salvation. Where we don't reject it out of hand it is often undermined by subtle suggestions that other things (morality or ritual) or other mediators can contribute to our salvation.

By affirming that redemption is found only through the sacrificial death of our Lord Jesus Christ we mean that God in no way takes our human merit into account when he forgives. The transformation of life that comes through Christ also comes to us through the propitiation (*i.e.* the turning away from us of God's holy wrath) made on our behalf by Jesus Christ our Lord. The holiness which the Holy Spirit produces in us is not itself a ground of acceptance with God: it is a consequence. We cannot become holy unless we have first received 'righteousness from God ... through faith in Jesus Christ' (Romans 3:22), *i.e.* we become holy because we have been forgiven, and not vice versa.

The outstanding truth to be grasped is that the death of Christ is 'the centre of gravity in the New Testament' (James Denney). Denney adds, 'Not Bethlehem, but Calvary, is the focus of revelation.' It is his death, not his life or teaching, which Christ himself commands us to remember in the Lord's Supper. On this we cannot compromise. As Denney goes on to say, 'If God has really done something in Christ on which the salvation of the world depends, and if he has made it known, then it is a Christian duty to be intolerant of everything which ignores, denies, or explains it away. The man who perverts it is the worst enemy of God and men.'

One of the ways in which the exclusive role of the Lord Jesus is distorted is the emphasis on the role of Mary and the 'saints', which has developed in the Roman Catholic Church. But the New Testament does not allow for any other mediator than the Lord Jesus, who died 'to bring you to God' (1 Timothy 2:5; 1 Peter 3:18). We respect Mary and the apostles for what they were and did, but they must not detract from the sufficiency of the Lord Jesus Christ. He is the *only* mediator.

What do we put behind us, as we conclude this chapter? We reject foolish optimism about the essential goodness of mankind. We do not accept that this world can progress into utopia. We do not accept any view of Christ's person or work that detracts from his full equality with God or from the uniqueness of the salvation he brings. We forsake trust in our own righteousness, in ritual or good works. 'Nothing in my hand I bring, Simply to thy cross I cling.'

We reject sentimentality, triviality or over-familiarity in our expressions of love and worship of the 'Lamb on the throne' (*cf*. Revelation 5:6, 13). Perhaps, too, we could look critically at how we speak about or to the Lord Jesus Christ. Do our singing and praying reflect the reverence with which the New Testament writers speak of him after his ascension? He is the Lord of glory.

Notes

1 John Stott, *The Cross of Christ* (IVP, 1986), pp. 202–203.
2 See the treatment of such passages in John Stott's book *The Cross of Christ* (IVP, 1986), and in Leon Morris' book *The Atonement* (IVP, 1983).

GOD'S WORK FOR US AND IN US

CHAPTER THREE

Justification

Justification as God's act of undeserved mercy, in which the sinner is pardoned all his sins, and accepted as righteous in God's sight, only because of the righteousness of Christ imputed to him, this justification being received by faith alone.

The word 'justification' has five syllables and sounds Latin and technical. This is enough for some people to assume that it is difficult and irrelevant, not to say unspiritual. But you cannot read far in Paul's letter to the Romans, for example, without realizing that to him it was the answer to our deepest problem – how to be right with God. What does it mean, then, and why is it so important?

A traveller was once lost in a strange country and stopped to ask a local man the way. The local thought for a while and then responded. 'It's difficult to explain. If I were you, I wouldn't start from here!' That is rather like our problem with understanding justification. Our late twentieth-century

Western culture has put us in the wrong place to start. If you go back to what we said earlier on man's sinfulness and guilt (chapter 2), you will see that we emphasized the difference between 'guilt' and 'guilt feelings'. The first speaks of our standing in relation to God's law, and is objective. That is, it exists outside ourselves and irrespective of our feelings on the matter. That is where we must begin in understanding justification. It is God's answer to our guilt, to our estrangement from him, to our condemnation because we have failed to keep God's law.

The 'wrong place' from which people start today, in understanding justification, is a lack of understanding of the fact of God's law, and of true guilt as distinct from guilt feelings. Paul, as a religious Jew, had a deep sense of God's law, because the Old Testament had taught that. But before his conversion, like many Jews then and since, Paul had got some aspects of the law out of proportion.

Justification is God's answer, then, to our guilt. It is a *legal* concept. (The word 'forensic' is sometimes used to express this.) It expresses what God does about my relationship to his law, not about the state of my heart. In that sense it is something which takes place *outside* me, not within.

Our present-day legal term 'acquittal' gives some idea of it, but it is too negative. An acquittal is a judicial pronouncement that the accused is 'not guilty'. It could mean simply that the jury were not able to come to a confident agreement on the facts! Justification is God's very positive declaration that we are 'accepted as just'. God declares that we are accepted by him.

The gospel's answer to my weak and corrupt heart is often called *sanctification* (although the biblical use of that word is wider than that). It is God's process, carried out by his Holy Spirit *within* the believer, of changing him into Christ's likeness. The process begins with his conversion, and is completed only at the end of his earthly life. Justification and sanctification are two very distinct truths, but they are inseparable in our experience. When God justifies a person he simultaneously begins the process of change. But it can save a great deal of doctrinal and pastoral confusion to get these terms clear in our thinking.

Someone has tried to set out these two truths in this way:

> The two are inseparable in fact, but they are distinguishable in thought ... Justification concerns our standing; sanctification our state. The former affects our position [before God]; the latter our condition. The first deals with relationship [to God]; the second with fellowship [with God]. Even though they are best wed together we must never confuse them. The one is the foundation of peace, 'Christ for us'; the other is the foundation of purity, 'Christ in us'. The one deals with acceptance [with God]; the other with attainment. Sanctification admits of degrees, we may be more or less sanctified; justification has no degrees, but is complete, perfect, and eternal.[1]

Mercy . . . pardon . . . by faith alone

The wonder of the Christian gospel is that justification is something given (as we might expect) not to those who deserve it (because none do) but to those who are unworthy! We do not deserve to be justified. Jesus made this point repeatedly when he said that he had not come to save the righteous, but sinners (*e.g.* Luke 5:32). But the idea would have been no surprise to the writers of the Old Testament (*cf.* Psalm 130:3, for example). The wonderful paradox of the gospel is that God saves the undeserving, not treating us as we deserve. The Doctrinal Basis puts this forcefully: it is 'God's act of undeserved mercy'. 'Mercy' is by definition undeserved! But the human heart is adept at blunting or evading the point. Hence the emphasis! It promises to the *sinner* the *pardon* of his sins. He is then *accepted* as righteous.

How can the God of truth and justice deal with sinners in this way? It seems to fly in the face of justice. We have already touched on this in the section on the death of Christ (chapter 2). But the wording here reminds us of Paul's great statement of the gospel as something by which a 'righteousness' such as God's law demanded is in fact provided. 'In the gospel a righteousness from God is revealed', he affirms (Romans 1:17). And after describing the plight of man without Christ he returns to that phrase in Romans 3:21–22: 'But now a righteousness from God, apart from law, has been made known ... This righteousness from God comes through faith in Jesus Christ to all who believe.' That great phrase recurs in Philippians 3:9:

'the righteousness that comes from God and is by faith'.

The wording of the Doctrinal Basis sees that righteousness as the positively holy and worthy character of the Lord Jesus Christ, which is imputed, or 'credited', to his people. The New Testament tells us not just that Jesus lived a sinless life but that it was a positively holy life, fully obedient to God. And the gospel tells us not only that *our* sin was punished in *Christ*'s death, but that we are treated by God as having his righteousness. That is fuller than mere forgiveness!

As the Dutch theologian Bavinck once put it, 'in grace He counts the righteousness of Christ as ours, so that we should fulfil to the full the justice of His law, should receive complete remission of all our sins, and obtain a confident entry into His heavenly Kingdom'.[2]

The emphasis on God's 'righteousness' as the basis of our salvation also carries with it the triumphant implication that because of Christ's work it is 'righteous' of God to forgive sinners. It is no uneasy subterfuge. So John declares that God is 'faithful and *just*' and will forgive us if we confess our sins (1 John 1:9). And this underlies the repeated Old Testament appeals to God for help, on the basis of his righteousness.

The final phrase of this section explains how we receive this mercy. The New Testament letters make it clear that we have no cause whatever for self-righteousness. God's saving grace is 'not by works', or 'not the result of your own efforts' (Ephesians 2:9, GNB). And our efforts make no contribution to it at all. We don't 'produce' anything – not even our faith – which is then rewarded by God. Saving faith is simply believing God's promises of salvation and entrusting ourselves to Christ to save us, abandoning all self-righteousness.

That is why the phrase 'by faith alone' is used. That doesn't mean that a Christian doesn't do good works; far from it. But we do them because we have been forgiven, and not in order to be forgiven. God's grace is accepted by us with what someone has called 'the naked hand of faith'. Jesus' story of the Pharisee and the tax collector says the same, 'This man [*i.e.* the one who simply asked for forgiveness without any pretence of goodness], rather than the other, went home justified before God' (Luke 18:14). A. M. Toplady's verse says it well:

> Nothing in my hand I bring,
> Simply to Thy cross I cling;
> Naked, come to Thee for dress;
> Helpless, look to Thee for grace;
> Foul, I to the fountain fly;
> Wash me, Saviour, or I die!

Obviously this truth is at the heart of the gospel, and the devil will do his best to keep its truths from men and women. People have replaced the simplicity and certainty of the gospel by ritualism or morality, keeping self-righteous people complacent and those who are conscious of sin, anxious.

Neglecting this truth also leads to depression and lack of assurance and peace even in true Christians. It is very clear in the New Testament that wrong or incomplete understanding of the truth not only affects our practice. Our emotional life also suffers. The writers put a great deal of emphasis on our being fully assured of our position before God. God wants us to be very sure of his love and his acceptance of us (Romans 8:31–39). And that is possible only when we are resting on his grace alone, received through faith alone.

Repentance and faith

The need for the Holy Spirit to make the work of Christ effective to the individual sinner, granting him repentance toward God and faith in Jesus Christ.

This clause asserts two main things. The first is that no-one can become a Christian by their own unaided will-power. And the second is that we consciously become a Christian by being brought to repentance and faith.

The Bible has strong things to say about human nature. One of its words to describe men and women without Christ is 'dead' (*e.g.* Ephesians 2:1, 5; Colossians 2:13). They are unresponsive, lifeless, impotent. 'No-one can say, "Jesus is Lord", except by the Holy Spirit', states Paul (1 Corinthians 12:3). And Jesus said: 'No-one can come to me unless the Father has enabled him' (John 6:65). Paul describes people without Christ as having their minds blinded by the god of this age so that they cannot see the light of the gospel (2 Corinthians 4:4). Clearly something significant is needed to bring us from death to life.

That great change is the work of the Holy Spirit.

Because of it, the Christian is described in the New Testament as one who is 'born again' (John 3:3) and has become a 'new creation' (2 Corinthians 5:17). This is contrasted with his previous condition in which he was 'dead in ... transgressions and sins' (Ephesians 2:1). This great change is an operation of the Holy Spirit (John 16:8–15; Acts 16:14; 1 Corinthians 2:10–12; Ephesians 2:1–10). It has been described as 'a radical and complete transformation wrought in the soul (Romans 12:2; Ephesians 4:23) by God the Holy Spirit (Titus 3:5), by virtue of which we become "new men" (Ephesians 4:14; Colossians 3:10), no longer conformed to this world (Romans 12:2; Ephesians 4:22–23), but in holiness and knowledge of the truth created in the image of God'.[3]

This great change is expressed in various dramatic phrases in the New Testament. We have been 'made alive' (Ephesians 2:5); God 'made his light shine in our hearts to give us the light of the knowledge of the glory of God in the face of Christ' (2 Corinthians 4:6); we 'were once darkness, but now ... light in the Lord' (Ephesians 5:8). Theologians refer to this change as God's 'effectual call', the work of the Holy Spirit which makes us Christians and gives us life (Acts 2:39; Romans 8:30; 1 Corinthians 1:24ff.). He normally uses the Scriptures (read, preached or remembered), leading us to awareness of sin, 'repentance to life' and saving faith in our Lord Jesus Christ (Ezekiel 36:26–27; John 3:1–21; 2 Corinthians 5:17; see also Romans 8 and Ephesians 1). And that brings us to the second main point of this clause.

See how the book of Acts describes the work of the

Spirit of Christ in the human heart and the human response: 'One of those listening was a woman named Lydia ... The Lord opened her heart to respond to Paul's message' (Acts 16:14). Until the Lord opens our hearts the work of Christ is of no value to us. When he does, and we respond in repentance and faith, we are 'born of God', and become God's children (1 John 5:1). We are translated into a new quality of life, and are new creations (2 Corinthians 5:17).

A person consciously becomes a Christian by receiving Jesus Christ as Saviour and Lord (John 1:12–13) not merely by becoming aware of the work of Christ. And the purpose of evangelism, in the same way, is not just to inform people but to see them come to personal repentance and faith. It is not enough for people to be looking for some purpose in life, or to be attracted by the person of Jesus. Repentance and faith are the keys. They are deliberate acts of the will (though only possible through the work of the Holy Spirit), and they focus on the person and work of Christ (see Acts 2:38; 3:19; 20:31).

Sanctification

The indwelling of the Holy Spirit in all those thus regenerated, producing in them an increasing likeness to Christ in character and behaviour, and empowering them for their witness in the world.

In a previous section we emphasized that God's work *for* us is not to be separated in experience from God's work *in* us.

69

We can never remind ourselves too often that the Christian is a 'new creation' (2 Corinthians 5:17). Paul tells us emphatically that the Holy Spirit lives in everyone who is a Christian (Romans 8:9, 14–16; 1 Corinthians 6:19), and his presence there is the God-given seal of his membership in the family of God (Ephesians 1:13–14).

a. '. . . an increasing likeness to Christ . . .'

What difference does it make to have the Holy Spirit within you? When we first become Christians we are sometimes conscious of a joy and a peace which is unlike anything we have known before. A conscience that has been cleansed is a wonderful thing. We may also find ourselves feeling and showing love to other Christians in a way we would not even have understood before. These are the results, the 'fruit' as Paul puts it, of the Holy Spirit within us (cf. Galatians 5:22–23).

But the list of that fruit, in Galatians 5, reads on. He does not stop at love and joy, and if we do there may be reason to doubt if the 'fruit' is genuine. In saving us God intends to make us more like Christ, not just to give us happiness (Romans 8:29; 2 Corinthians 3:18). In Galatians 5 Paul goes on to list the qualities of that life which the Spirit is producing in us.

This is the outworking of being 'born again', which is what regeneration really means. The phrase 'born again' has become devalued and people often use it as a vague expression for 'becoming a Christian'. But it means that we have received a new kind of life from God, a life that will grow. The

Spirit's work is to cause this growth, and also to teach and convict us so that we realize our need of it, and co-operate in achieving it.

Because it is a process of growth it takes time. It will not be completed in this life. And because it is a process of change in a sinful nature that is not removed when we become Christians it involves deep-seated conflict (*cf.* Galatians 5:16–17). The Christian finds he is not free from sinful thoughts, and may often meet temporary defeat in the war with evil. We shouldn't be surprised at this, and certainly shouldn't be discouraged. The process is painful but we are not alone in it.

God's dealings with us are very individual. He treats us each in our own way. Some make steady progress, while others have ups and downs. Some have deep emotional crises along the way which others don't experience. Christians have sometimes fallen into the trap of making one particular experience into a standard for everyone, and the result of this has been several varieties of 'second blessing' teaching. (This is the view that we need not only to be converted but also to have a further crisis experience to be able to live effective Christian lives.) Sadly, these can bring some people under severe pressure, and lead into unnecessary discouragement and even despair. In particular, they often wrongly suggest that we can live our Christian lives free from any defeat or trouble.

It is wonderful freedom to be able to have our own walk with God, shaped by his Word and not by the tastes and preferences of others.

Perhaps these words from the Westminster

Confession of Faith can be food for thought as we close this section:

> This sanctification is throughout in the whole man, yet imperfect in this life; there abideth still some remnants of corruption in every part: whence ariseth a continual and irreconcilable war; the flesh lusting against the Spirit, and the Spirit against the flesh. In which war, although the remaining corruption for a time may much prevail, yet, through the continual supply of strength from the sanctifying Spirit of Christ, the regenerate part doth overcome; and so the saints grow in grace, perfecting holiness in the fear of God.[4]

b. '. . . empowering them for their witness in the world'

God's sanctifying process moves certainly towards the goal of our being fully Christlike (Romans 8:29; Philippians 1:6). But that shouldn't let us think of our lives on earth as being like seedlings in a greenhouse, quietly growing, out of sight, until the time comes for us to be planted out. It is true that this world is 'the *present* evil age', (Galatians 1:4), due to be replaced at the end of the age by God's perfect recreation of heaven and earth. (See 2 Peter 3:13; 2 Corinthians 4:18.) Meanwhile, however, there is work to be done and Christians must resist the temptation to take monastic refuge away from the normal life of this world. Christ calls *us* 'the light of the world' (Matthew 5:14–16), meant to be seen, and 'the salt of the earth' (Matthew 5:13), meant to

72

have an influence in a decaying culture. Paul urges the Philippians to 'shine like stars' among the people of 'a crooked and depraved generation' (Philippians 2:15; see GNB translation); Titus is told to encourage slaves to live 'so that ... they will make the teaching about God ... attractive' (Titus 2:10).

There is work for God's people to do in virtually every part of the life of this world, including parts which Christians have sometimes neglected or even avoided. And it is work for which the Holy Spirit gives us power (Acts 1:8). We are not alone in it, nor are we limited to our own human resources.

Notes

1 W. H. Griffith Thomas, *The Principles of Theology* (1930).
2 H. Bavinck, *Our Reasonable Faith*, translated by H. Zylstra (Baker Book House, Grand Rapids, 1977), p. 457.
3 Quotation from B. B. Warfield.
4 Chapter XIII (Sections ii and iii) of the Westminster Confession.

THE CHURCH AND CHRIST'S SECOND COMING

The Church

The one holy universal church, which is the Body of Christ, and to which all true believers belong.

In the last chapter we concentrated on the work of the Holy Spirit in the individual. In God's plan of salvation, however, that is inseparably connected to his work in the church. In coming to Christ in repentance and faith we are united to the whole body of all true Christians past and present. So as Paul describes the individual Christian as the 'temple of the Holy Spirit' (1 Corinthians 6:19) he can also apply the expression to the whole church (1 Corinthians 3:16). There he probably has the congregation in Corinth in mind, but he also speaks of the universal church as a 'holy temple in the Lord . . . a dwelling in which God lives by his Spirit' (Ephesians 2:21–22). ✓

Denominations there may be, and divisions, whether caused by pride and personality cults or by deeply held and unresolvable differences of belief. But all who come to Christ in personal saving faith and acknowledge him as Lord are made, by their new relationship with him, members of the one, sanctified, world-wide company of his redeemed people (John 10:16; 1 Corinthians 1:2). For the Spirit of God who gives them new life in Christ, unites them in him with all who are similarly baptized by the one Spirit (1 Corinthians 12:13). This community is a body of which Christ is the Head (Ephesians 1:22–23). It is a priesthood to offer the sacrifice of worship (1 Peter 2:5). This 'people of God' has the duty to spread the wonderful knowledge of God's saving work (1 Peter 2:9). In this community they are inter-dependent, as members of a body, and 'each member belongs to all the others' (Romans 12:5). They are intended to enjoy the fullness of their new life in Christ in active fellowship together. In this way they should preserve, and openly express, a unity which is God-given and already theirs in Christ (Ephesians 4:3, 13–16). Such fellowship is clearly meant to be experienced, wherever possible, by every Christian through active membership in a local congregation (Hebrews 10:24–25).

We live in a very individualistic culture. And when we become Christians we are still influenced by it. It shows itself in many ways. For example, many of our churches seem to operate on the 'bus' model. We sit in our seats, aware more of the minister, the 'driver', than of others around us, listening to what he says, finally getting out and going home! We may notice the other 'passengers' and talk to them without realizing the one life that unites us. 'One body ... one Spirit ... one Lord' (Ephesians 4:4–5).

What a poor response to the true nature of Christ's church! Paul makes much of the image of the body. He emphasizes that the parts of the body need one another and that each has a role to play for the benefit of the others. Christ through the Holy Spirit gives different gifts to different members for this purpose (Romans 12:3–8; 1 Corinthians 12:4–11; Ephesians 4:11–13). There is no such thing as a self-sufficient Christian. We depend on Christ, of course. But in his building of his church we also need one another.

Particularly in the Christian Unions, there is another trap we can fall into in our thinking about the church of Christ. We may realize the bond that unites all true Christians. We may gladly accept the task of joint witness to Christ in our college or university. But we can easily come to think of the Christian Union as our local congregation or church during our student days.

But Christian Unions have a limited purpose in a limited sphere and for a limited period in the experience of their members. They provide opportunities for fellowship and Bible study for Christian students who are temporarily thrown together during one important period of their lives. They are also centres of evangelistic witness with the same limitations. But their members should not neglect regular participation in the worship and fellowship of a proper local congregation, an expression of the

Body of Christ. Christian students ought normally to be baptized members, and to partake regularly of the Lord's Supper, in a local congregation. And they need to be well enough known to its spiritual leaders for them to be able to exercise proper pastoral care.

The leaders of UCCF are most emphatic that UCCF and the CUs that make it up are not churches. Churches often find it difficult to reach people in academic communities, and students have incomparable opportunities for reaching fellow students. We in UCCF see ourselves as an auxiliary to the mainstream of church life, helping Christian students in their witness in the academic community. We believe it is the duty and privilege of CU members to encourage one another to work in true communion with any Christian congregation which is scriptural in preaching and practice, and where members acknowledge the one Lord and confess the one faith.

From the very beginnings of UCCF it has been true that the Doctrinal Basis has been sincerely affirmed by individual members of many different denominations. Denominational differences have not been allowed to weaken the united witness. This has been a valuable feature of the work; it would be tragic if it were ever to become impossible.

So all CU leaders and members are urged to concentrate on the fundamental truths and to avoid divisions on denominational or similar issues. The Doctrinal Basis should express both the CU's narrowness and its breadth. United emphasis on the basic truths will be all the more effective if we can agree to differ on secondary matters. And when we place an unbalanced emphasis on secondary questions we almost always end up by neglecting the fundamentals.

Christians rightly often work to increase co-operation not only between local congregations but also between denominations (often called churches, although the New Testament doesn't use the word in that way). When we do this we give expression to our privilege and duty of fellowship with other Christians (see Acts 2:42). But as we do this we should remember that the New Testament gives no encouragement to us to exalt 'fellowship' at the expense of faithfulness to biblical truth. That is one of the painful realities of life for the Christian today, not least in the student world.

Christ's second coming

The future personal return of the Lord Jesus Christ, who will judge all men, executing God's just condemnation on the impenitent and receiving the redeemed to eternal glory.

During the last hundred years or so men and women came to feel that the world was permanent and steadily advancing. The Christian idea that God is in control of history and is going to bring it to an end was ridiculed. Even some within the Christian church were infected by this unbelief. No doubt people's natural aversion to any idea of final judgment was part of this.

Perhaps today, with our awareness of the dreadful possibilities of a nuclear holocaust, and with all the evidence of the futility of human society, people are less blindly optimistic. But in any case the Bible is clear that things do not just go on for ever; God will bring this world to an end and usher in his final perfect order of things. And it is also clear that that event is one of great significance for every man and woman who has ever lived. It will herald the final judgment.

The Bible is equally clear on that. Sin has to be accounted for, and a holy God cannot simply ignore mankind's rebellion against him. The universe would be a fearfully immoral place if he did. Jesus and all his apostles make that point very clear. We shall all have to give an account of ourselves at the judgment seat of Christ (2 Corinthians 5:10). And whatever may or may not be clear about the details of the final state, the words especially of Jesus himself make it clear that it is an indescribably awful thing for those who reject him, and wonderful beyond description for those he has redeemed.

The great event which will signal the end of the world is the return of the Lord Jesus Christ. This will be dramatic, visible and personal (*e.g.* Acts 1:11). Christians have not always agreed on the details of interpretation of the biblical material on this, and we are warned about getting uselessly side-tracked on points which are not clear. In particular, we are told that we cannot know the exact time of his return (Matthew 24:36; Mark 13:32–33). The main point is that he will surely come, and that we are to be watchful and ready, to be diligent and pure in our lives. (See Matthew 24:42; Mark 14:62;

John 14:3; 1 Thessalonians 4:13–18; 2 Thessalonians 1:7–10; 2 Peter 3:11–12; 1 John 3:2–3).

The promise of his personal return is as certain as his first coming. But unlike the obscurity of his first coming, the second will be an event of cosmic importance. And it will be sudden. It will be as lightning flashing across the sky (Matthew 24:27; Luke 17:24). It will be 'with power and great glory' (Matthew 24:30; Luke 21:27); after it there will be no further opportunity of receiving the blessings of the gospel (Matthew 25:10–12), and all must appear before the judgment seat of God (Romans 14:10; 2 Corinthians 5:10).

This last point is unpalatable to men and women, in the twentieth-century as in all ages, and today the Christian comes under strong pressure to evade or dilute it. In particular, in today's society we are pressed to accept that all religions are equally valid, and all lead to God. But it is not compassionate to mankind or honouring to God to avoid the fact of God's final judgment or its eternal significance to those who accept or reject God's gracious salvation through Christ alone.

The Christian finds encouragement and joy at the thought of Christ's coming. We shall be in the immediate presence of our Saviour. We shall enjoy the completion of our salvation in body and soul. We shall at last see the coming of God's perfect kingdom. No wonder that it should spur us on to holiness and service (2 Peter 3:11–14; 1 John 3:2–3). No wonder that John cried out 'Come, Lord Jesus' (Revelation 22:20)!

THE DEMANDS OF THE TRUTH

a. Believing the truth

Is that too obvious? Of course truth is to be
believed. Yet we can easily overlook the fact that
belief is always going to be one of the areas of the
devil's attacks. He attacks both Christians and non-
Christians on this point, directly and indirectly. He
brings against us the sudden fierce onslaught of a
new doubt, a new objection, or a new intellectual
difficulty. He distracts us with other pressures of
life, until a previously loved truth has become dis-
tant and unreal, and in the end easily jettisoned or
ignored.

So our first response to the truth is to remember
that it comes from God, and is to be believed. He
has spoken and we dare not neglect what he has
said (*cf*. Hebrews 2:3). This is part of our spiritual
warfare; we need to pray that the Holy Spirit will
enlighten our minds and keep us from the evils of
denial, confusion or neglect. We are also to be ready
to take trouble to understand the truth of the Bible.
God calls us to put in effort and study to hear what
he is saying in his Word.

b. *Responding to the truth from the heart*

God did not make us as intellectual machines. We often overstate the difference between what our modern jargon calls the 'cognitive' (the mind) and the 'affective' (the emotions). The Bible does not support that. The words 'mind' and 'heart' are used almost interchangeably in the Bible. We should respond with the whole person.

That is why we may find it more helpful to speak of 'applying' the truth rather than simply 'putting it into practice'. Our first application is to our own minds and hearts, before we start doing anything. We respond first by letting it affect our attitudes, our feelings, our motives.

If we rush to mechanical obedience without first letting God's truth soften, humble and motivate us we can become cold and formal Pharisees. God's way of speaking to us is that 'the imperatives of the New Testament are always well supported with incentives'.[1] We should meditate on the truths so that these incentives catch fire in our hearts. After all, the Bible is not an impersonal textbook of propositions but the message for the living God to his human creatures and his children. Through it we come to know God better, not as an abstraction but as the living Father, with whom we have fellowship.

Hans Burki comments:

It is imperative . . . to remain constantly vigilant against mere abstract thinking which reduces biblical doctrines to general principles which are easily handled by man without dependence on God. If Scripture bids us see what one cannot see

(2 Corinthians 4:18), to understand what is beyond understanding (Ephesians 3:19), to experience what surpasses our own emotional possibilities (Philippians 4:7), we are made aware that unenlightened human reason and emotion alone cannot comprehend God's revelation. Every type of knowledge can easily lead to pride. He who thinks that he knows something, does not know how to know. He who loves God is known by Him (1 Corinthians 8:1–3). Does our study of Scripture lead us to a knowledge that is related to love, to a love that fuses heart and mind? Does it lead to praise, prayer and practice? In order to combine knowledge with love, balance study with praise, we can ... transform each statement of the Doctrinal Basis (once we have studied it in Scripture) into a written prayer.[2]

Listen to the words of Martin Luther, as quoted by Burki:

No one can understand God or His Word who has not received such understanding directly from the Holy Spirit. But no one can receive it from the Holy Spirit without experiencing, proving and feeling it. In such experiences the Holy Spirit instructs us as in His own school, outside of which naught is learned save empty words and idle fables ... *Sola experientia fecit theologum* (only experience makes a theologian). Experience is necessary for the understanding of the Word. It is not merely to be repeated and known, but also to be lived and felt.[3]

Burki goes on to comment: 'It is a word against the Scribes of all times who glory in dead orthodoxy and a plea for valid personal experience authenticated by the Holy Spirit through the written Word.'[4]

c. Witnessing to the truth

The message of the Bible tells us that God has spoken, that man and the devil resist the message, and that it must be made clear so that men and women may repent and believe. To know the truth brings an obligation to make it known.

It is easy for us to take too much for granted in this. We can vaguely hope that truth will prevail, without our doing anything about it. But there have been long periods in history when the powers of darkness seemed almost to have put out the light. It was rekindled and the people of God could move forward again only when he raised up faithful and self-sacrificial men and women who cared enough to suffer for the sake of the truth. The Christian church has been rich in such men and women – saints, reformers and martyrs. And we in our turn must 'hold firmly to the faith' today (see Hebrews 4:14).

The gospel comes down to each new generation as God raises up people who are able to teach us. Paul told Timothy to find those who were reliable and competent teachers, to pass on the things Timothy had learned from Paul (2 Timothy 2:1–2; see also 1 Timothy 1:18; 6:13, 20). In our generation such 'reliable men' are still needed, who will be able 'to teach others'.

One of Paul's favourite metaphors to describe this responsibility to hand on the essentials of the tradition is that of keeping the 'deposit'. So 1 Timothy 6:20 might accurately be translated, 'Timothy, guard the deposit'. When Paul wrote these words the greater part of the 'deposit' had been communicated orally. We have it now in written form so that we may be in no doubt about its reliability and may avoid being confused by subsequent false traditions. There is today as much need as ever for us in our turn to hold fast to the treasure of the gospel and to hold it out to others.

d. Obeying the truth

From beginning to end the Bible presents its message to us in order to change us. God did not give us his Word to be read and studied, only to be put back on the shelf. To Paul, receiving the gospel can be described as 'the obedience that comes from faith', and unbelievers as those who 'do not obey the gospel' (Romans 1:5; 2 Thessalonians 1:8). And our Lord prayed that the Father would 'sanctify [his people] by the truth' (John 17:17).

God's truth has practical significance. And every aspect of our lives must come under the authority of God's Word, which gives us all the light we need. The use of the word 'obey' tells us that we shall sometimes find it difficult to do what God requires. It will require effort. This is where our calling Jesus 'Lord' is put to the test! That title implies that he has authority to rule and command. So he warns us that we must deny ourselves, and take up the cross and follow him, if we want to be his disciples (Matthew

16:24). That will not always be easy or comfortable.

This obedience is to be *total*. We do not have the right to bargain with God, or to select the areas of our obedience. We are not our own: we are Christ's. The privilege of belonging to him brings with it that high calling.

Obedience is the key to effective witness. Inconsistent living destroys the credibility of what we say about Christ. Consistent living, on the other hand, doing what God commands rather than what we prefer, is something the world finds strange. Men and women may be intrigued by it, or they may feel rebuked and react with hostility. But by God's grace the quality of our lives may win them over. (*Cf.* 1 Peter 4:4; John 3:19–20; 1 Peter 3:1–2). Many students first begin to think seriously about the gospel when they are struck by the lives of their Christian friends.

Paul saw himself as one who had the tremendous honour of being 'approved by God to be entrusted with the gospel' (1 Thessalonians 2:4). In our own way, we too have that privilege as his servants. May God help us all to fulfil that trust and bring the gospel of the Lord Jesus Christ to our fellow men and women in their great need of a Saviour.

Notes

1 R. C. Lucas, *The Message of Colossians and Philemon: fullness and freedom (Bible Speaks Today*, IVP, 1980), p. 140.
2 Hans Burki, *Essentials* (International Fellowship of Evangelical Students, 1975), p. 18.

3 *Essentials*, p. 15.
4 *Essentials*, p. 15.
5 *Essentials*, pp. 14–15.
6 *Essentials*, p. 14.

APPENDIX

The main branches of the Christian church have, historically, had more agreement on the fundamental truths than we might think. This is particularly true of the early church creeds such as the Apostles' Creed. And within the churches of the Reformation, many of the differences on basic doctrines have come in over the past two centuries as people have been less rooted in the Bible. There is more agreement on the basics than people suppose.

Summaries of the most important aspects of Christian truth have been in circulation from an early period in the Christian era. The best known examples are the Apostles' Creed and Nicene Creed. These emphasize the Persons of the Holy Trinity, particularly of the Lord Jesus Christ. The sixteenth-century Reformation produced several statements, and in these the focus shifts to include statements about the way of salvation. Examples of these are the Thirty-nine Articles of the Church of England (1571) and the Westminster Confession of Faith (1647). The Westminster Confession was designed to unite the Churches of England and Scotland, and has remained the 'subordinate standard' of the Church of Scotland and the majority of the Presbyterian Churches ever since. Modified versions were prepared by the early Congregational Churches (Cambridge, 1648, and Savoy, 1680) and Baptist

Churches (1689). The changes that were made relate essentially to denominational distinctives and not the foundational gospel truths which they all had in common. The first Methodist Churches retained the Thirty-nine Articles of the Church of England as their doctrinal standard, together with the standard edition of Forty-four Sermons of John Wesley and his Notes on the New Testament. In other parts of the world and in succeeding centuries other summaries of Christian belief have appeared. In the case of a number of independent Baptist Churches and Assemblies of Brethren, many have adopted no detailed doctrinal statement but are content with a reference to the teaching of the Bible as a whole. Nonetheless, within such groups there has usually been a strong consensus on the fundamental elements of the gospel.

How do these statements of faith compare with the Bible? Those who formulated them believed that our human minds alone cannot discover God or his truth. We depend on him to take the initiative to reveal himself. He has revealed something of himself in the world of creation, but supremely in the Bible. There alone we learn those things which are able to make us 'wise for salvation' (2 Timothy 3:15). The Scripture is the sum total of revealed truth in relation to God. The creeds and confessions are secondary standards – valuable but fallible attempts to summarize its main teachings. If ever we come to treat them as equal in authority to the Bible we completely distort their purpose. They are meant to be 'subordinate' standards.

These summaries of Christian teaching are

usually in some systematic form. The Bible itself is not all written in that way: there is also teaching by example, through historical event, through poetry and in other ways. If God in his wisdom has given us a Bible with this rich variety of form, we would be wise to follow the Bible's own method of approach and never allow it to be displaced in our learning by any other book or method. But a systematic summary helps us by giving a balanced expression of Scripture's teaching.

FURTHER READING

The following booklist is to encourage all who use this booklet to read more about Christian beliefs. It is not intended to be complete, nor is it a list for theological students, but has in mind the needs of younger Christians who have little present knowledge of the subject.

1 Introductory

Boice, J. M. *Foundations of the Christian faith* (IVP, 1986)
Milne, B. *Know the truth* (IVP, 1982)
Packer, J. I. *God's words* (IVP, 1981)
Stott, J. R. W. *Basic Christianity*, second edition (IVP, 1971)

2 Systematic theology

Bavinck, H. *Our reasonable faith* (Baker Book House, 1977)
Berkhof, L. *Systematic theology*, sixth edition (Banner of Truth, 1971)
Davis, J. J. *Let the Bible teach you Christian doctrine* (Paternoster, 1985)
Kuiper, R. B. *The Bible tells us so* (introductory) (Banner of Truth, 1968)

3 Holy Scripture

Balchin, J. *Let the Bible speak* (IVP, 1981)

Bruce, F. F. *The New Testament documents*, fifth edition (IVP, 1960)

Edwards, B. H. *Nothing but the truth* – an explanation of the inspiration and authority of the Bible (Evangelical Press, 1978)

4 Bible study aids

Bridgland, C. and Foulkes, F. *Pocket guide to the Bible* (IVP, 1988)

Douglas, J. D. and others *New Bible Dictionary*, second edition (IVP, 1982)

Fee, G. D. and Stuart, D. *How to read the Bible for all its worth* (Scripture Union, 1983)

Green, Joel *How to read the Gospels and Acts* (IVP, 1986)

Green, Joel *How to read prophecy* (IVP, 1987)

Guthrie, D. and others *New Bible Commentary*, third edition (IVP, 1970)

Longman, T. *How to read the Psalms* (IVP, 1988)

Stibbs, A. (ed.) *Search the Scriptures*, fifth edition (IVP, 1967)

Willoughby, R. (ed.) *Start here* (IVP, 1988)

Willoughby, R. (ed.) *Growing with God* (IVP, 1988)

Willoughby, R. (ed.) *Meeting with God* (IVP, 1987)

Also two series of books on the individual books of the Bible:

Tyndale Commentaries – detailed introduction and commentary (IVP)

The Bible Speaks Today – exposition and application (IVP)

5 The person and work of Christ

Olyott, S. *Son of Mary, Son of God* (Evangelical Press, 1984)

Sproul, R. C. *Who is Jesus?* (Scripture Union, 1986)

Stott, J. R. W. *The cross of Christ* (IVP, 1986)

Wells, D. F. *The Person of Christ* (Marshall, Morgan and Scott, 1985)

6 The Holy Spirit and Christian living

Bridge, D. *Signs and wonders today* (IVP, 1985)

Green, E. M. B. *I believe in the Holy Spirit* (Hodder, 1985)

Hallesby, O. *Prayer* (IVP, 1948)

Huggett, J. *Living free* (IVP, 1984)

White, J. *The fight* (IVP, 1977)

7 The second advent

Grier, J. W. *The momentous event* (Banner of Truth, 1970)

Ladd, G. E. *Blessed hope: a biblical study of the second advent and the rapture* (Eerdmans, 1956)

Travis, S. H. *I believe in the second coming of Jesus* (Eerdmans, 1987)

8 The Church

Barclay, Ian *What Jesus thinks about the church* (Kingsway, 1986)

Jones, R. T. *The great Reformation* (IVP, 1985)

Kuiper, R. B. *The glorious body of Christ* (Banner of Truth, 1983)

Renwick, A. M. and Harman, A. M. *The story of the church*, second edition (IVP, 1985)